Nutrition recommendations for TCM - Stomach - Qi deficiency

Please check these recommendations always with a nutrition consultant, therapist, doctor or dietician. The recipes and the list of ingredients are supporting the conventional medical therapy. The calorie disclosures of fresh ingredients (fruit and vegetables) vary according to quality and time of harvest. The contents were checked by a dietician and a nutrition consultant for the Traditional Chinese Medicine (TCM).

Author:
©2020 Josef Miligui
www.ebns.at

Source:
The lists are created from the EBNS database for nutritional counseling. The database is used by dietitians, therapists and doctors for advising the patient / client.

Literature:
The specialist literature and the training documents of the German and Austrian dietary and traditional Chinese medicine serve as a knowledge base. We have used the documents as a basis of knowledge, adapted it to our experience and completed them.
http://nutribook.info/

Production and publishing:
BoD – Books on Demand, Norderstedt
ISBN: 9783750410053

Diet recommendations for TCM - Stomach - Qi deficiency

1 Treatment strategy

Strengthen stomach and spleen Qi.
Warm and neutral YES, hot and refreshing LITTLE, cold NO

2 Avoid

Too hot or cold food and drink, Raw food, Carbonated drinks, Late night food, Chaotic or NonStop eating (buffet)

3 Breakfast

4 Snack

5 Lunch

6 Afternoon

7 Dinner

8 Any time

9 Recipes

(rec.) = You can use more.
(little) = You should use less than specified
(omit) = omit.

9.1 8 treasures of rice

Strengthens kidney and bladder, builds up Qi, strengthens the spleen, repels moisture, reduces internal heat, prevents cancer, builds heart, calms nerves.
Cooking time approx. 1 hour
Calories p. portion: 212
4 portions

Quantity of ingredients
Lily bulbs 1 table spoon / 5g. () - cool - sweet, bitter .... *
Longane 1 table spoon / 5g. (little) - warm - sweet .... *
King Solomon's-seal 1 table spoon / 5g. () - neutral - sweet, bitter .... *
Yam root, yam root tuber 1 table spoon / 5g. () - neutral - sweet .... *
Coix (seeds) YiYi Ren 1 table spoon / 5g. (little) - cool - sweet, neutral .... *
Rice wild (nature rice) 1 1/2 cups / 240g. (yes) - neutral - sweet, bitter ..... metal
Water 8-10 cups / 800g. (yes) - cool - salty .... earth

Cooking instructions:
Each one 1 tbsp: Bai He, Longan, Yu Zhu, Da Zao, Shan Yao, Lian Mi, Yi Yi Ren, Qian Shi
Add hot water and soak for about 30 minutes. Then add 1 - 2 cups of rice (normal) and simmer for 1/2 to 1 hour until the rice is very soft. Or: Cook for about 3 hours with the herbs a congee. Then the herbs do not have to be soaked.

9.2 Basic recipe for a chicken broth worming

Strengthens Qi and blood, is very warm.
Cooking time approx. 2-3 hours
Calories p. portion: 90
9 portions
Allergens: L

Quantity of ingredients
Chicken meat 1/2 piece / 600g. (little) - warm - sweet.............................. wood
Carrot 2 pieces / 150g. (rec.) - neutral - sweet..earth
Leek 1 stick / 45g. (little) - warm - acrid.. metal
Celery root 1 piece / 500g. (rec.) - cool - sweet...earth
Ginger fresh 2 slices / 2g. (rec.) - warm - acrid .... metal
Juniper berry 1 teaspoon / 3g. (yes) - warm - sweet, acrid, bitter.................fire
Bay leaf 3 pieces / 2g. () - warm - acrid.. *
Water 4 cup / 900g. (yes) - cool - salty...earth

Cooking instructions:
Remove chicken parts from fat. Place chicken pieces in a saucepan
with hot water and heat till it boils briefly, skimming any resulting foam.
Add coarsely chopped vegetables and all spices and cook over medium
heat for 2 to 3 hours. Strain the finished soup. Throw away vegetables
and bones.
Tip: If you want to use the meat as a soup insert, take out after 45
minutes and return only the bones in the soup.
Refrigerate for later use.

9.3 Basic recipe for a reissue soup (Congee)

Warms the stomach and spleen, harmonizes the intestine, forces Qi,
reduces moisture.
Cooking time approx. 2-4 hours
Calories p. portion: 140
3 portions

Quantity of ingredients
Rice variety any 1 cup / 120g. (yes) - warm - sweet................................ metal
Water 6 cups / 700g. (yes) - cool - salty ....earth

Cooking instructions:
Cook rice and water in a ratio of about 1: 6. The amount of water
determines the thickness of the mash (matter of taste).
Put the rice in a saucepan with a heavy lid. It is important to simmer the
rice after a short boil on the slightest flame, otherwise it burns.

Boil the rice for 2-4 hours. The longer he cooks, the more he strengthens.

If you want to eat the dish for breakfast, you can put the rice on just before bedtime.

To be on the safe side, you should first check the behavior of your pot and cooker under observation for a similar amount of time, so that nothing burns. Refrigerate for later use.

9.4 Basic recipe for a vegetable soup, nutritious

Strengthens spleen and lung, regulates Qi flow, builds up Qi, dries out, passes downwardly, strengthens stomach Qi.
Cooking time approx. 2-3 hours
Calories p. portion: 48
5 portions
Allergens: L

Quantity of ingredients
Olive oil 1 table spoon / 4g. (little) - cool - sweet ....earth
Onion white 1 piece / 60g. (little) - warm - acrid .... metal
Carrot 3 pieces / 200g. (rec.) - neutral - sweet...earth
Parsnip 3/8 lbs - 6oz / 150g. (rec.) - cool - bitter ....fire
Celery root 1 cup / 100g. (rec.) - cool - sweet ....earth
Ginger fresh 1/2 teaspoon / 2g. (rec.) - warm - acrid............................... metal
Lemon 1/2 piece / 25g. () - cold - sour.. wood
Juniper berry 6 pieces / 6g. (yes) - warm - sweet, acrid, bitter ....fire
Thyme dried 1 pinch / 1g. () - warm - bitter .... metal
Lovage 1 table spoon / 3g. (yes) - warm - acrid, bitter .... metal
Lovage 1 table spoon / 3g. (yes) - warm - acrid, bitter .... metal
Bay leaf 2 leaves / 1g. () - warm - acrid.. *
Salt 1 pinch / 1g. (rec.) - cold - salty... water
Water 3 cups / 650g. (yes) - cool - salty ....earth

Cooking instructions:
Cut the vegetables into cubes.
Heat oil in hot pot, fry shortly onions and vegetables.
Add cold water, then add ginger, bay leaf and lemon juice.
Season with juniper, thyme and lovage. Cover for 2 - 3 hours on a low heat and simmer.
The used vegetables should be thrown away.
The basic recipe serves as a soup base and to refine vegetables, legumes or cereals.
If you want to eat vegetable soup immediately, add the desired vegetables half an hour before.
Refrigerate for later use.

9.5   Beef soup with carrots, leeks, bay leaves

Strengthens spleen Qi, strengthens blood and Qi, moisturizes, relaxes, builds up Qi, spreads, strengthens spleen and liver, regulates Qi flow, strengthens stomach Qi.
Cooking time approx. 2-3 hours
Calories p. portion: 194
5 portions

Quantity of ingredients
Beef meat 1 lbs / 500g. (little) - warm - sweet ....earth
Carrot 2 pieces / 200g. (rec.) - neutral - sweet ....earth
Leek 1/2 piece / 150g. (little) - warm - acrid .... metal
Bay leaf 3 leaves / 1g. () - warm - acrid.. *
Corn Grease (Polenta) 1 table spoon / 10g. (rec.) - neutral - sweet...........earth
Water 2 cup / 450g. (yes) - cool - salty..earth
Salt 1 pinch / 0,5g. (rec.) - cold - salty ....water

Cooking instructions:
In a saucepan with water (enough to cover the meat), add beef soup meat or leg slice and simmer for a moment; then pour off the broth, rinse the meat with hot water (this will save you from foaming), clean the pot and put the meat in hot water again; add chopped carrot, leek, corn and bay leaf; simmer until the meat is cooked.

9.6   Black-eyed beans stew

Strengthens spleen and kidney, is very nutritious, warms the stomach and spleen, harmonizes the intestine, forces Qi, strengthens stomach and kidney, strengthens spleen and kidney.
Cooking time approx. 20 min
Calories p. portion: 140
5 portions

Quantity of ingredients
Black-eyed peas 1 cup / 100g. (yes) - neutral - sweet, acrid....................water
Rice variety any 1 1/2 cups / 200g. (yes) - warm - sweet..........................metal
Water 10 cups / 1000g. (yes) - cool - salty...earth

Cooking instructions:
Soak the beans overnight and strain.
In a ratio of 1: 2, simmer the beans together with the rice in the Water. Depending on how hot the flame is and how thin the dish should be, more water must be added. Variation: Add vegetables fried in oil, such as carrots, celery tubers, onions or leeks.

9.7 Carrot and rice gruel soup

Warms the stomach and spleen, harmonizes the intestine, forces Qi, reduces moisture, strengthens spleen and liver, regulates Qi flow, moisturizes, relaxes, builds up Qi, spreads.
Cooking time approx. 10 min
Calories p. portion: 101
1 portions

Quantity of ingredients
Basic recipe for a rice soup (Congee) 1 cup / 120g. (rec.) - neutral - sweet..... *
Carrot 2 pieces / 100g. (rec.) - neutral - sweet..earth
Salt 1 teaspoon / 4g. (rec.) - cold - salty..water

Cooking instructions:
Peel and grate carrots. Heat the rice soup (according to the basic recipe) till it boils and add the grated carrots and salt. Cook for 10 minutes.

9.8 Celery juice

Strengthens stomach Qi, moisturizes, relaxes, builds up Qi, spreads.
Cooking time approx. 5 min
Calories p. portion: 33
1 portions
Allergens: L

Quantity of ingredients
Celery root 1/2 piece / 200g. (rec.) - cool - sweet......................................earth
Water 1 cup / 120g. (yes) - cool - salty...earth
Salt 1 pinch / 0,5g. (rec.) - cold - salty...water

Cooking instructions:
Peel celeriac and cut into pieces and juice. Mix with water and salt as needed.

9.9 Chicken soup with angelica root and buckthorn fruit

Strengthens spleen and nourishes the blood and Yin of the liver, forces Qi and blood, is very warming.
Cooking time approx. 1 1/2 hours
Calories p. portion: 77
3 portions
Allergens: LO

Quantity of ingredients
Basic recipe for a chicken soup (warming) 2 cup / 500g. (yes) - warm - *........ *
Bocksdorn fruits (Fructus Lycii, Goji, goji berry dried 1/8 lbs - 2oz / 50g. () - cool - wood

Cooking instructions:
When you cook chicken broth according to basic recipes add angelica root and willowberry fruits in the last 40 minutes.

Ingestion: Drink 2-3 cups of broth daily.

9.10 Clear soup from goose

Forces spleen, stomach and lungs, relieves weakness, forces Qi, calms the stomach, gets Qi moving, directs upwards, strengthens spleen and liver, regulates Qi flow, moisturizes, relaxes, builds up Qi, spreads.
Cooking time approx. 2-3 hours
Calories p. portion: 334
6 portions

Quantity of ingredients
Goose parts 1,1 lbs / 500g. (yes) - neutral - sweet.....................................metal
Carrot 1 piece / 100g. (rec.) - neutral - sweet..earth
Onion (shallot) 1 piece / 25g. (little) - warm - acrid, sweet.........................metal
Leek 1 piece / 250g. (little) - warm - acrid ....metal
Parsley 1 Twig / 4g. (yes) - warm - bitter...wood
Lovage 1 Twig / 4g. (yes) - warm - acrid, bitter ....metal
Water 4 cup / 1000g. (yes) - cool - salty...earth
Salt 1 pinch / 0,5g. (rec.) - cold - salty...water

Cooking instructions:
Simmer goose pieces with vegetables and herbs for 2-3 hours. Sift through a fine cloth and cool. Degrease and store in the refrigerator.

9.11 Kidney bean pot with lamb and sage

Nourishes Yin from heart and kidney, strengthens spleen and kidney Yang, forces Qi, heats middle and lower heater, dissolves stagnation, directs upwards, moisturizes, relaxes, builds up Qi, spreads.
Cooking time approx. 1 1/2 hours
Calories p. portion: 391
4 portions
Allergens: F

Quantity of ingredients
Soybean oil 3 table spoons / 30g. (yes) - warm - sweet............................earth
Onion white 2 pieces / 120g. (little) - warm - acrid ....metal
Lamb meat 5/8 oz / 200g. (little) - warm - sweet ....fire
Sage 4-5 leaves / 2g. (little) - neutral - bitter, spicy ....fire
Salt 1 pinch / 0,5g. (rec.) - cold - salty..water
Rosemary 1/2 teaspoon / 2g. (yes) - warm - bitter ....fire
Thyme 1/2 teaspoon / 2g. (rec.) - warm - bitter .... *
Kidney beans (red) 5/8 lbs - 8oz / 250g. () - neutral - sweet.....................water
Water 3 cups / 750g. (yes) - cool - salty..earth

Cooking instructions:
Soak kidney beans in water overnight and strain.
In a saucepan with oil, roast the onion. Dice the lamb and place in the pot.
Season with salt, sage, rosemary and thyme.
Roast lamb well and cover pot. Cook over low heat and add ten-quarters of a gallon (750ml.) of cold water after 10 minutes.
Salt again.
Heat till it boils. Add beans to it.
Simmer for at least 1 hour until the beans and meat are tender.

9.12 Kuzu soup in the morning

Moisturizes, relaxes, builds up Qi, spreads, forces stomach, harmonizes middle, reduces internal heat, detoxifies, softens, passes downwardly.
Cooking time approx. 5 min
Calories p. portion: 12
1 portions
Allergens: E

Quantity of ingredients
Water 1 cup / 250g. (yes) - cool - salty...earth
Soy sauce 1 dash / 2g. () - cold - salty ....water
Umeboshi paste 1 knife tip / 2g. () - warm - sour......................................water

Cooking instructions:
Mix kuzu with cold water and heat till it boils while stirring. Once it is glassy, remove from heat and let cool. Season
with Tamari and Umeboshipaste or crushed umeboshi plums

There is always the possibility to support your stomach and intestines with this recipe, taken before the right breakfast.
A morning cure for stomach and mucous membranes. Fix the base balance.

9.13 Millet with egg and butter

Forces blood, Yin and Jing, nourishes Yin, moisturizes in case of internal dryness, forces blood, forces spleen, calms nerves and stomach, strengthens spleen and kidney, diuretic, strengthens Qi and kidney Jing, moisturizes, relaxes, builds up Qi, spreads
Cooking time approx. 25 min
Calories p. portion: 338
2 portions
Allergens: CG

Quantity of ingredients
Millet 1 cup / 100g. (little) - cool - sweet, salty ....earth
Ginger fresh 1/2 teaspoon / 1g. (rec.) - warm - acrid .... metal
Salt 1 pinch / 0,5g. (rec.) - cold - salty .... water
Parsley 2 table spoons / 16g. (yes) - warm - bitter .... wood
Pepper powder (hot) 1 pinch / 1g. () - warm - bitter ....fire
Chicken egg 2 pieces / 100g. (yes) - neutral - sweet .... earth
Butter organic 2 table spoons / 20g. (yes) - neutral - sweet .... earth
Nutmeg 1 pinch / 0,2g. () - warm - acrid .... metal
Water 1 1/2 cups / 200g. (yes) - cool - salty .... earth

Cooking instructions:
Simmer the millet with the ginger and nutmeg in the water for 5 min. and let it swell for another 30 min.
Cook and peel 1 soft egg per person; pile up the millet on plates and place 1 egg each in a hollow in the millet mountain; Put butterflakes over it. Sprinkle with chopped parsley and the rose paprika.

9.14 Mung bean stew

Dissipates excess heat, is very nutritious, reduces heat and poison, softens, passes downwardly, warms the stomach and spleen, harmonizes the intestine, forces Qi, reduces moisture.
Cooking time approx. 2 hours
Calories p. portion: 665
2 portions

Quantity of ingredients
Mung bean 5/8 lbs - 8oz - 500g / 300g. () - cool - sweet, salty..................water
Sunflower oil 3 table spoons / 30g. (little) - cool - sweet ....earth
Amaranth 1/2 teaspoon / 2g. (yes) - neutral - bitter, sweet...........................fire
Cumin (Caraway seed) 1/2 teaspoon / 2g. (yes) - warm - acrid ....metal
Coriander 1/2 teaspoon / 2g. (rec.) - warm - acrid....................................metal
Rice round grain 1/2 cup / 60g. (yes) - neutral - sweet.............................metal
Water 3 cups / 300g. (yes) - cool - salty...earth
Ginger fresh 1 inch / 3g. (rec.) - warm - acrid...metal
Kombu seaweed (Saccharina japonica) 1 inch / 2g. () - cold - salty..........water
Salt 1 pinch / 0,5g. (rec.) - cold - salty..water
Parsley 1 table spoon / 3g. (yes) - warm - bitter......................................wood

Cooking instructions:
Soak mung beans overnight.
Heat sunflower oil in a hot pot. Stir in the amaranth, fennel seeds, cumin and coriander and fry briefly.
admit basmati rice, some ginger and mung beans and roast briefly.
Pour water and heat till it boils.
Add a piece of kombu alga and salt.
Simmer for 1-1/2 hours.
Garnish with parsley or coriander.

9.15 Polenta with peach

Strengthens blood and fluids, brings blood into motion, builds up Qi, spreads, strengthens stomach Qi, diuretic, moisturizes, relaxes, builds up Qi, spreads, warms the stomach and spleen, promotes blood circulation and conduction flow, relieves cold-sick
Cooking time approx. 20 min
Calories p. portion: 197
3 portions

Quantity of ingredients
Water 1 1/2 cups / 240g. (yes) - cool - salty...earth
Corn Grease (Polenta) 1 cup / 120g. (rec.) - neutral - sweet....................earth

Peaches 2-3 pieces / 400g. (yes) - warm - sour, sweet...........................earth
Vanilla pod 1 pinch / 1g. () - neutral - sweet.................................... *
Chili (pod or ground) 1 pinch / 0,1g. (little) - hot - acrid .... metal
Cinnamon ground 1 pinch / 1g. (little) - hot - acrid, sweet...................... *

Cooking instructions:
Pour the polenta into a pan of hot water with constant stirring until the polenta has the desired consistency. Pull the polenta from the fire and let it soak for 10 minutes.

Wash fresh peaches and cut into quarters. Pour into the finished polenta the peaches, add the vanilla and add Chili
to taste, stir and let it go for 3 minutes.

Winter varieties: Pickled fruit, pear, apples

9.16 Pumpkin soup

Forces lungs and spleen, diuretic, forces Qi, protects liver, forces Qi, forces spleen, relieves inflammation, moisturizes, relaxes, builds up Qi, spreads, strengthens spleen and liver, regulates Qi flow, moisturizes, relaxes, builds up Qi, spreads.
Cooking time approx. 1 hour
Calories p. portion: 105
3 portions

Quantity of ingredients
Pumpkin 3/4 lbs / 300g. (rec.) - warm - sweet..earth
Carrot 2 pieces / 100g. (rec.) - neutral - sweet..earth
Potato 2 pieces / 120g. (yes) - neutral - sweet..earth
Olive oil 1 table spoon / 10g. (little) - cool - sweet......................................earth
Onion white 1 piece / 50g. (little) - warm - acrid .... metal
Water 1 cup / 120g. (yes) - cool - salty..earth
Parsley 1 table spoon / 7g. (yes) - warm - bitter... wood
Anise (Common Fennel) 1 pinch / 1g. (rec.) - warm - acrid.......................earth
Salt 1 pinch / 1g. (rec.) - cold - salty... water

Cooking instructions:
Add the olive oil to the pan, add the diced pumpkin, diced carrots and potatoes. Roast them shortly, add the finely chopped onion, fill with water, add enough water to cover the vegetables at least 3 finger-widths. Boil at low heat.
Season with sea salt, add small cutted parsley, a pinch of anise (little). Allow to simmer for about 35 minutes. Then purée the soup and add some water, depending on the consistency of the soup.

9.17 Quick flakes with compote or jam

Forces Qi, dries out, passes downwardly, strengthens middle heater, moisturizes, relaxes, builds up Qi, spreads, strengthens kidney Qi, essence and brain, forces kidney, warms the middle.
Cooking time approx. 5 min
Calories p. portion: 189
2 portions
Allergens: H

Quantity of ingredients
Quinoa 5-7 table spoons / 50g. (yes) - neutral - sweet, sour........................fire
Water 1 cup / 250g. (yes) - cool - salty...earth
Walnuts 1 table spoon (grated) / 8g. (yes) - warm - sweet.........................earth
Olive oil 1 table spoon / 10g. (little) - cool - sweet...................................earth
Honey 2 table spoons / 20g. () - cold - sweet..earth
Vanilla 1 pinch / 0,2g. (rec.) - neutral - sweet..*
Anise (Common Fennel) 1 pinch / 0,2g. (rec.) - warm - acrid....................earth
Cardamom 1 pinch / 0,2g. () - warm - acrid...*
Chili (pod or ground) 1 pinch / 0,1g. (little) - hot - acrid ....metal

Cooking instructions:
Put the quinoa flakes in a pan and add water. Boil for 3-5 minutes, pull from the fire, add nuts and compote. Add a dash of oil. Sweeten as needed with honey, whole cane sugar or agave syrup.
Spices and aromas: vanilla, anise, fennel or coriander, cardamom, a little chili.
Winter: apple compote, pear compote, fruit jam.
Summer: plum compote, apricot compote.

9.18 Quick zucchini soup

Reduces mucus, preserves the fluids, cools liver fire, forces stomach Qi.
Cooking time approx. 10 min
Calories p. portion: 42
4 portions

Quantity of ingredients
Zucchini 2-3 pieces / 500g. (little) - cool - sweet ....earth
Onion white 1 piece / 50g. (little) - warm - acrid ....metal
Corn germ oil 2 table spoons / 6g. () - neutral - sweet ....earth
Parsley 1 table spoon / 7g. (yes) - warm - bitter...................................... wood
Chives 1 teaspoon / 3g. (little) - warm - acrid ....metal
Water 2 cup / 400g. (yes) - cool - salty..earth

Cooking instructions:
Fry chopped onion in oil. Add sliced zucchini and sauté well. Pour with water. Chop parsley and chives, add and puree everything.

9.19 Quinoa with peach

Strengthens blood and fluids, brings blood into motion, builds up Qi, spreads, forces Qi, dries out, passes downwardly, strengthens middle heater, moisturizes.
Cooking time approx. 20 min
Calories p. portion: 248
2 portions

Quantity of ingredients
Quinoa 1 cup / 100g. (yes) - neutral - sweet, sour ....fire
Water 1 1/2 cups / 240g. (yes) - cool - salty...earth
Honey 2 teaspoons / 4g. () - cold - sweet...earth
Peaches 2 pieces / 240g. (yes) - warm - sour, sweet.............................earth
Linseed oil 2 teaspoons / 4g. () - neutral - sweet...................................earth
Lemon Balm (fresh) 1 teaspoon (chopped) / 1g. () - cool - sour...............metal
Chili (pod or ground) 1 pinch / 0,1g. (little) - hot - acrid ....metal
Cinnamon ground 1 pinch / 0,2g. (little) - hot - acrid, sweet ....*
Vanilla 1 pinch / 0,2g. (rec.) - neutral - sweet...*

Cooking instructions:
In the evening: Put quinoa in hot water and boil soft, covered 15 to 20 minutes.
In the morning: Warm up quinoa with 1 tablespoon water.
Steam lightly Peaches in a saucepan or add them fresh. Decorate with fresh lemon balm.
Summer: nectarines, apricots
Winter: Pickled fruit, pear, apples

9.20 Reissue soup with fresh fruits

Forces kidney and bladder, strengthens Qi and kidney Jing, moisturizes, relaxes, builds up Qi, reduces internal heat, produces humors, moisturizes, spreads, expels cold, dissolves stagnation, drives sweat, stimulates nerves.
Cooking time approx. 1 1/2 hours
Calories p. portion: 143
4 portions
Allergens: G

Quantity of ingredients

Rice wild (nature rice) 1 cup / 100g. (yes) - neutral - sweet, bitter .... metal
Water 8 cups / 900g. (yes) - cool - salty .... earth
Apple (sweet) 1 1/2 cups / 200g. (little) - cool - sweet, sour .... earth
Butter organic 1 table spoon / 10g. (yes) - neutral - sweet .... earth
Vanilla 1 pinch / 0,2g. (rec.) - neutral - sweet .... *
Chili (pod or ground) 1 small pinch / 0,1g. (little) - hot - acrid .... metal
Sugar cane sugar 2 teaspoons / 6g. (little) - cool - sweet .... earth

Cooking instructions:

Prepare rice congee according to basic recipe.

At the end, add finely chopped fruits to the season, vanilla, chili and butter; sweet to taste.

Variant: With nuts, the dish can always be made richer and more filling.

Effect: Cooked or steamed fruits are easier to digest and act better than raw. For some fruits, which are particularly suitable for hot summer days - such as melons and berries - it is still advisable to add the fruits only to a hot porridge.
Other types of fruit - such as apples, pears, plums and cherries - can also be simmered for a while.

9.21 Rice congee with carrots and fennel

Nutritious builds up Qi, forces the digestive functions.
Cooking time approx. 2 hours and more
Calories p. portion: 131
3 portions
Allergens: G

Quantity of ingredients

Basic recipe for a rice soup (Congee) 2 cup / 500g. (rec.) - neutral - sweet..... *
Carrot 2 pieces / 100g. (rec.) - neutral - sweet .... earth
Fennel 1 piece / 250g. (rec.) - warm - sweet, little acrid .... earth
Butter organic 1 teaspoon / 3g. (yes) - neutral - sweet .... earth
Cardamom 1/2 teaspoon / 1g. () - warm - acrid... *

Cooking instructions:

Cook rice congee according to basic recipe.
Clean and cut carrots and fennel.
When carrots and fennel are cooked from the beginning, they serve

wholesomeness. If added shortly before the end of the cooking time, taste and vitamins are retained.
Refine with butter and cardamom before serving.

9.22 Rice congee with crushed walnuts

Nourishing and slightly warming, warms the middle, builds up Qi, warms the stomach and spleen, harmonizes the intestine, forces Qi, reduces moisture.
Cooking time approx. 2 hours and more
Calories p. portion: 406
2 portions
Allergens: H

Quantity of ingredients
Basic recipe for a rice soup (Congee) 4 cups / 500g. (rec.) - neutral - sweet... *
Sugar cane sugar 2 table spoons / 20g. (little) - cool - sweet.....................earth
Walnuts 1 cup / 70g. (yes) - warm - sweet ....earth
Cinnamon ground 1 pinch / 0,2g. (little) - hot - acrid, sweet .... *

Cooking instructions:
Cook the basic recipe for rice soup (congee)
Note: The crushed walnuts can be cooked from the beginning.
Variation: Refine with sweet or spicy ingredients as you like. In particular, cinnamon, cloves, and ginger increase the warming effect and wholesomeness.

9.23 Rice congee with dried fruit

Warms the stomach and spleen, harmonizes the intestine, forces Qi, reduces moisture, nourishes blood and Yi, harmonizes lungs Qi, strengthens Qi and kidney Jing, moisturizes, relaxes, builds up Qi, spreads.
Cooking time approx. 10 min
Calories p. portion: 210
2 portions
Allergens: GO

Quantity of ingredients
Basic recipe for a rice soup (Congee) 4 cups / 500g. (rec.) - neutral - sweet... *
Butter organic 1/2 teaspoon / 5g. (yes) - neutral - sweet............................earth
Apricot dried 6 table spoons / 50g. () - warm - sweet ....earth
Water 1/2 cup / 50g. (yes) - cool - salty..earth
Maple syrup 1 dash / 3g. () - cool - sweet ....earth

Cooking instructions:
Cook rice congee according to basic recipe.

Melt a small amount of butter over a low heat and briefly fry small dried fruit with 1/2 cup of water. Add the amount
of rice porridge desired for the meal and heat. Serve hot and sweeten with maple syrup if necessary.
Variant: In addition fresh fruit with braise.

9.24 Rice dulse soup

Strengthens spleen and liver, regulates Qi flow, relaxes, builds up Qi, spreads, dries out, passes downwardly, strengthens stomach Qi, warms the stomach and spleen, harmonizes the intestine, forces Qi, reduces moisture.
Cooking time approx. 5 min
Calories p. portion: 190
2 portions
Allergens: L

Quantity of ingredients
Basic recipe for a rice soup (Congee) 4 cups / 500g. (rec.) - neutral - sweet... *
Basic recipe for a vegetable soup (nutritious) 2 cup / 500g. (rec.) - neutral - *. *
Dulse (seaweed) 2 table spoons / 15g. () - neutral - salty .... water

Cooking instructions:
Worm up a portion of pre-cooked basic recipe for a ricesoupe (congee) and a portion pre-cooked basic recipe for a vegetable soup.
Bake the dulse in the oven at 220 degrees for 3 minutes. Spread the crisp dulse over the rice.

9.25 Rice with berries

Preserves the fluids, contracts, forces kidney and bladder, moisturizes intestines, nourishes blood and Yi, cools heat, distributes mucus, derives wind-cold and wind-heat, brings the stomach Qi in motion, solves congestion.
Cooking time approx. 5 min
Calories p. portion: 160
4 portions
Allergens: N

Quantity of ingredients

Rice wild (nature rice) 1 cup / 120g. (yes) - neutral - sweet, bitter .... metal
Water 6 cups / 700g. (yes) - cool - salty .... earth
Sunflower seeds 2 table spoons / 20g. (yes) - neutral - sweet .... earth
Sesame, white 2 table spoons / 18g. () - neutral - sweet .... earth
Berries of the season 1 cup / 120g. () - neutral - sweet, sour .... wood
Vanilla 1 pinch / 0,2g. (rec.) - neutral - sweet .... *
Peppermint 2 leaves (chopped) / 2g. () - cool - acrid, bitter .... metal
Anise (Common Fennel) 1 pinch / 1g. (rec.) - warm - acrid .... earth

Cooking instructions:

Warm 2 ladles of boiled rice congee according to basic recipe. Add
sunflower seeds or sesame seeds. Serve in a bowl, sprinkle with fresh
berries. Sweetening as needed.

Spices: vanilla, fresh mint, anise

Summer: plum (tastes good with grated nutmeg)
Winter: pickled cherries, grated apple, jam with a lot of fruit content.

9.26 Rice with parsnips

Regulates Qi, dries out, passes downwardly, warms the stomach and
spleen, harmonizes the intestine, forces Qi, reduces moisture.
moisturizes, relaxes, builds up Qi, spreads. distributes mucus, activates
Wei Qi, forces Qi.
Cooking time approx. 45 min
Calories p. portion: 206
3 portions

Quantity of ingredients

Rice variety any 1 cup / 120g. (yes) - warm - sweet .... metal
Water 1 1/2 cups / 200g. (yes) - cool - salty .... earth
Salt 1 pinch / 1g. (rec.) - cold - salty .... water
Parsnip 3-4 pieces / 450g. (rec.) - cool - bitter .... fire
Olive oil 1 table spoon / 10g. (little) - cool - sweet .... earth
Sage 1 teaspoon / 3g. (little) - neutral - bitter, spicy .... fire

Cooking instructions:

Peel the parsnips and cut into slices. Fry for a short time in oil. Add the
rice and fry again for a short time. Add the water and cook it at least 30
min. Sprinkle with fresh chopped sage.

9.27 Roasted oatmeal with grapes compote

Moisturizes, relaxes, builds up Qi, spreads, forces Qi, warms the stomach and spleen, promotes blood circulation and conduction flow.
Cooking time approx. 25 min
Calories p. portion: 328
2 portions
Allergens: AO

Quantity of ingredients
Oat flakes roasted 1 cup / 120g. () - warm - sweet....................................metal
Grapes red 1 1/2 cups / 240g. (little) - cool - sweet...................................earth
Ginger fresh 1/2 teaspoon / 1g. (rec.) - warm - acrid...............................metal
Raisins 2 table spoons / 20g. (little) - warm - sweet.................................earth
Cinnamon ground 1 pinch / 1g. (little) - hot - acrid, sweet..............................*
Water 1 1/2 cups / 200g. (yes) - cool - salty..earth

Cooking instructions:
Roast the oats briefly, pour over water, add raisins and cook while stiring for 20 min. Add grapes, ginger and cinnamon.

9.28 Spelled-grid porridge with berries of the season

Nourishes fluids, moisturises dryness, produces humors, moisturizes intestines, cools inner heat, preserves the
 fluids, contracts, forces middle, nourishes heart and liver-blood, preserves the fluids, contracts.
Cooking time approx. 15 min
Calories p. portion. 244
2 portions
Allergens: AGH

Quantity of ingredients
Cow's milk (1.5% fat) 1/2 cup / 125g. (little) - neutral - sweet.....................earth
Water 1/2 cup / 125g. (yes) - cool - salty...earth
Spelled semolina 5 table spoons / 50g. (rec.) - neutral - sweet................wood
Butter organic 2 teaspoons / 20g. (yes) - neutral - sweet...........................earth
Berries of the season 1/4 lbs - 4oz / 100g. () - neutral - sweet, sour.........wood
Honey 1-2 teaspoons / 5g. () - cold - sweet...earth
Almond 1-2 teaspoons / 5g. () - neutral - sweet.......................................earth
Peppermint 3-4 leaves / 2g. () - cool - acrid, bitter...................................metal
Cinnamon ground 1 pinch / 0,5g. (little) - hot - acrid, sweet...........................*
Vanilla 1 pinch / 0,2g. (rec.) - neutral - sweet..*
Cocoa 1 pinch / 0,5g. (little) - warm - sweet, bitter......................................fire
Coconut grated 1 table spoon / 10g. (little) - warm - sweet........................earth

Cooking instructions:
Stir in spelled semolina in cold water and boil slowly over medium heat. After boiling, remove from the heat and let
 simmer for a few minutes. Depending on the desired consistency, some water may have to be added. Stir in the butter and fine grated nuts in the mash and raspberries. Serve with honey or whole-grain sugar as desired.
Spices and aromas: fresh mint, cinnamon or vanilla, cocoa, coconut

Summer: raspberries, blueberries, strawberries

9.29 Tea from anise

Warms the middle, forces stomach and spleen, warms stomach, reduces cold-evil, harmonizes stomach-Qi, warms kidney.
Cooking time approx. 15 min
Calories p. portion: 3
4 portions

Quantity of ingredients
Anise (Common Fennel) 1 teaspoon / 3g. (rec.) - warm - acrid.................earth
Water 2 cup / 500g. (yes) - cool - salty..earth

Cooking instructions:
Heat the water till it boils and put it aside. Add anise.
10 min. to let go.
Pour through a tea strainer. Sweet to taste with honey.

In order to achieve a salutary effect, you should drink 2 cups of anise tea per day.

9.30 Tea from ginseng

Forces heart, lungs, stomach, spleen, kidney-Qi.
Cooking time approx. 20 min
Calories p. portion: 0
4 portions

Quantity of ingredients

Water 2 cup / 500g. (yes) - cool - salty...earth
Ginseng tea 4g, (2 teabag) ....*

Cooking instructions:
A very mild form of taking ginseng is achieved by placing it in a thermos of hot water. You can also use the root several times, not just for a pot filling. Ideally, you should have cooked the water for 10 minutes - it is then assigned to the conversion phase of fire (TCM) - and to use non-carbonated medicinal spring water, if the quality of the water on site is not good.

Ingestion: This mild ginseng tea can be drunk throughout the day for strengthening.

9.31 Tea from Longane

Forces spleen, builds up lung, builds up heart, calms nerves.
Cooking time approx. 10 min
Calories p. portion: 0
4 portions

Quantity of ingredients

Longane 2 teaspoons / 4g. (little) - warm - sweet...*
Water 2 cup / 500g. (yes) - cool - salty...earth

Cooking instructions:
Heat the water till it boils and put it aside. Add Longane and 10 min. to let go. Sweet to taste with honey. Strain when pouring.

9.32 Tea from thyme

Converts mucus, forces lungs and spleen, dries out, passes downwardly.
Cooking time approx. 10 min
Calories p. portion: 0
4 portions

Quantity of ingredients

Thyme 3 table spoons / 6g. (rec.) - warm - bitter...*
Water 2 cup water / 500g. (yes) - cool - salty ....earth

Cooking instructions:
Heat the water till it boils and put it aside. Add thyme and 10 min. to let go. Strain. Sweet to taste with honey.
Drink 2 to 3 cups daily by mouth

9.33 Tea mixture against intestinal inertia

Cools liver fire, removes internal heat, has a decongestant effect, forces stomach.
Cooking time approx. 20 min
Calories p. portion: 1
8 portions

Quantity of ingredients
Gentian root 1 table spoon / 20g. () - cold - bitter... *
Water 4 cup / 1000g. (yes) - cool - salty...earth

Cooking instructions:
Preparation:
Mix gentian 20 g kalmus 20 g and blackthorn 20 g.

Preparation: 1 tablespoon of the mixture to 1 cup as an infusion, let stand for 15-20 minutes.
Use: Drink 1 cup warm in the morning and evening.

9.34 Vegetable miso soup with tofu

Strengthens spleen and liver, regulates Qi flow, moisturizes, relaxes, builds up Qi, spreads, forces Qi, forces liver and kidney, reduces damp heat, detoxifies, nourishes fluids, reduces internal heat, dries out, passes downwardly.
Cooking time approx. 15 min
Calories p. portion: 107
4 portions
Allergens: EN

Quantity of ingredients
Sesame oil 2 table spoons / 35g. (little) - cool - sweet ....earth
Onion (shallot) 1 piece / 20g. (little) - warm - acrid, sweet........................ metal
Carrot 1 piece / 70g. (rec.) - neutral - sweet...earth
Leek 2 inches / 10g. (little) - warm - acrid... metal
Water 3 cups / 750g. (yes) - cool - salty...earth
Endive salad 2 table spoons / 30g. () - neutral - bitter..................................fire

Soy Tofu 2 table spoons / 30g. (rec.) - cool - sweet ....earth
Ginger fresh 1/2 teaspoon / 1g. (rec.) - warm - acrid..............................metal
Miso 2 table spoons / 15g. (rec.) - neutral - salty ....water

Cooking instructions:
In sesame oil first sauté onions, then carrots and a little leek; Pour in
water and simmer gently; add the bean sprouts and endive leaves and
leave to stand; Tofu cubes, add a little ginger; at the end stir in a little
cooled cooking-water the Miso.

9.35 Warming porridge

Forces Qi and defensive power.
Cooking time approx. 10 min
Calories p. portion: 357
1 portions
Allergens: AHO

Quantity of ingredients
Oat flakes (whole grain) 6 table spoons / 60g. (rec.) - warm - sweet ....metal
Fig dried 3 pieces / 15g. (yes) - warm - sweet...earth
Star anise 1 piece / 1g. (yes) - warm - acrid...*
Ginger fresh 1 pinch / 0,5g. (rec.) - warm - acrid.....................................metal
Water 1 cup / 120g. (yes) - cool - salty...earth
Maple syrup 1 table spoon / 10g. () - cool - sweet.....................................earth
Walnuts 1 table spoon (chopped) / 8g. (yes) - warm - sweet ....earth

Cooking instructions:
Soak the dried fruit. Roast Oatmeal dry. Add dried ginger, star anise or
cinnamon, a little grated ginger and boil everything with water to a
mash. With maple syrup sweet. Whip grated walnuts and sprinkle
before serving.

Effect: Suitable for the cold season.
Caution: Fresh ginger does not drink over a long period of time.

10 Effects of food

10.1 Use ingredients: recommendable

Anise (Common Fennel)
Basic recipe for a duck soup
Basic recipe for a fish soup
Basic recipe for a rice soup (Congee)
Basic recipe for a vegetable soup (nutritious)
Black caraway
Carrot
Carrot (Early Carrot)
Carrot juice without sugar
Celery root
Coriander
Corn Grease (Polenta)
Fennel
Fennel tea
Ginger fresh
Gourd
Ground

Ground caraway
Miso
Oat flakes (whole grain)
Oat fusion (baby food)
Parsley root
Parsnip
Pumpkin
Rice Basmati
Salt
Soy Tofu
Spelled semolina
Sweet potato
Thyme
Turmeric (yellow root)
Turnips
Umeboshi plums (Japanese apricots)
Vanilla

10.2 Use ingredients: yes

Amaranth
Apricots
Arrowroot
Basic recipe for a beef soup
Basic recipe for a beef soup (warming)
Basic recipe for a chicken soup (warming)
Basil
Basil (fresh)
Bitter melon
Black tea
Black-eyed peas
Boxhorn clover seeds
Breadcrumbs (wheat bread, bread roll)
Butter organic
Carp
Celery sticks
Chervil
Chestnuts
Chicken egg
Clove
Coconut flakes
Cod
Couscous
Cumin (Caraway seed)

Dates dried
Dill
Fig
Fig dried
Fish pieces mixed (fresh water)
French beans
Goose
Goose parts
Grass carp
Hawthorn
Hazelnuts
Herbs various
Hyssop
Juniper berry
Kohlrabi
Kumquats
Lentils
Lentils black
Lentils red
Lentils yellow
Lovage
Marjoram
Mediterranean fish (cod, plaice, haddock, sea eel, mackerel)
Morel (black, dried)

Multi-grain bread (gray bread)
Mustard seeds
Oat flour
Octopus
Okra
Oregano dried
Papaya
Parsley
Peaches
Peaches (canned)
Peanut oil
Peas
Peppers
Peppers (rose peppers)
Perch
Pheasant
Pine nuts
Pistachios
Plaice
Poppy
Potato
Pumpkin seed oil
Pumpkin seeds
Quinoa
Radish black
Rapeseed oil
Rice (fragrance)
Rice (Gaoliang / Sorghum)
Rice (whole grain)
Rice black
Rice flour

Rice long grain rice
Rice malt
Rice mash
Rice noodles
Rice red
Rice round grain
Rice starch
Rice sticky
Rice sweet
Rice variety any
Rice wild (nature rice)
Rose hip tea
Rosemary
Sake
Salmon
Savory
Sesame paste (Tahini)
Sour milk cheese 20%
Soybean oil
Soybeans, black
Soybeans, yellow
Spiny lobsters
Star anise
Sunflower seeds
Vanilla powder
Walnuts
Water
Water hot
Wheat semolina
Wheat semolina for children
White bread (wheat bread)

10.3 Use ingredients: little

Adzuki beans
Apple (sour)
Apple (sweet)
Apple juice (natural cloudy)
Apricot
Artichoke
Aubergine
Balm
Barley
Beef bone marrow
Beef fillet
Beef heart
Beef heart (calf)
Beef meat
Beef meat (calf)
Beef meatbones
Beef Oxtail pieces
Beef soup meat
Beer (Pils)
Beer (Top-fermented German dark

beer)
Broccoli
Brussels sprouts
Buckwheat
Bulgur (cereals)
Buttermilk
Calamari
Cashews
Cauliflower
Cereal coffee
Chard
Cherry
Cherry juice
Chicken meat
Chickpeas
Chili (pod or ground)
Chinese cabbage
Chives
Cinnamon ground
Cinnamon sticks

Clementines
Cocoa
Coconut grated
Coconut milk
Coffee
Coix (seeds) YiYi Ren
Cow's milk (1.5% fat)
Cow's milk (whole milk 3.5% fat)
Cream, sweet 30%
Cress
Curcuma
Curd cheese 20%
Curd cheese 40%
Deer meat
Deer meat
Duck (heart)
Duck (slaughtered)
Elderberry blossom tee
Feta cheese
Fresh cheese
Ginger powder
Goat
Goat and sheep's milk
Goat cheese
Grapes red
Lamb bones
Lamb meat
Leek
Lemon peel
Longane
Lychee
Lychee in Preserved
Margarine
Margarine (diet)
Millet
Millet flakes
Mozzarella
Oat
Olive oil
Olives
Onion (shallot)
Onion (spring onion)
Onion read

Onion white
Oysters
Parmesan
Peanuts
Pear
Pear juice
Peas, green
Pepper white (ground)
Pomegranate
Pork skin
Quail
Quail egg
Quince
Rabbit meat
Raisins
Red cabbage
Rye
Rye flour
Sage
Salsify
Savoy cabbage / kale
Sesame oil
Soybean milk
Spelled (Dark) bread
Spelled grain
Spelled wholemeal flour
Spinach
Sugar brown
Sugar candy white
Sugar cane sugar
Sugar fructose - fruit sugar
Sugar glucose - grapes sugar
Sugar Milk Sugar
Sunflower oil
Tarragon (Estragon)
Turkey breast meat
Vegetable juice
Wheat flour
Wheat germ oil
White cabbage
Wild boar meat
Zucchini

10.4 Do not use contra-acting foods

Agar agar (kelp)
Asparagus (green or white)
Avocado
Bamboo shoots
Banana
Banana (cooking banana)
Boletus mushroom
Burdock root tea

Carambola (Star fruit)
Champignon
Chanterelle
Crab
Cranberry
Cranberry juice
Cucumber
Currant (black)

Currant (red)
Currant (white)
Curry
Dandelionroots tea
Garlic
Gooseberry
Grapefruit (Pomelo)
Grapefruit juice
Kefir
Kiwi
Lemon
Lemon juice
Lime
Mallow (Malva sylvestris) blossom tea
Mango
Mineral water
Miso paste (soy bean paste)
Mold cheese
Morel, dried
Mulberry fruit
Mullet
Mussels
Mutton
Nutmeg
Orange
Orange juice
Oyster mushroom
Pepper Cayenne
Peppercorns
Pickle
Pimento
Pineapple

Pineapple (from a can)
Pineapple juice without sugar
Plum
Pork meat
Rabbit liver
Radish
Radish (white, green, purple-red)
Reishi mushroom
Rhubarb
Sauerkraut (cutted cabbage fermented)
Seacrab
Shiitake, dried
Sorrel
Sour cherries
Sour cream 15% fat
Sour milk
Soy sauce
Spirit
Strawberries
Strawberry Juice
Sugar white
Tangerine
Tomato
Vinegar (Apple vinegar)
Vinegar (Red wine vinegar)
Vinegar Aceto Balsamico
Watermelon
Wild strawberries
Yarrow tea
Yogi tea
Yogurt (natural, 1.5% fat)
Yogurt (natural, 3.5% fat)

11 Complementary

11.1 Acorus root

Acorus calamus, rhiz.
Preparation: Different effects
Strengthens spleen-qi and stomach-qi, warming, draining moisture.
Distributes cold mucus from the spleen, stomach and lungs.
Strengthening Jing.
Average daily dose: 1-5g infus, decoction drug or 1-8ml tincture.

11.2 Caraway

Carum carvi
Preparation: Healing tea (infusion)
Warms spleen qi and stomach-qi, strengthens yang spleen, kidney and heart. Moves lung-qi.

11.3 Cardamom

Elettaria cardamomum
Preparation: Decoction
Warms the middle, releases stagnation, leads upwards. Tonifies kidney yang, warms kidneys and spleen; strengthens stomach, astringent.
Decoction from 3-10 g, drink in two doses on an empty stomach
Do not use on: stomach ulcers
Active ingredients: fatty oil, sugar, protein, gum, starch, many other ingredients.

11.4 Centaurium (centaury)

Centaurium, herb.
Preparation: Healing tea (infusion)
Clarifies stomach heat, dries moisture. Tonifies Spleen-Qi and Stomach-Qi, moves Liver-Qi and Intestinal-Qi. Derives moisture-heat and heat.
Pour 2 teaspoons of the tea into 250 ml of boiling water and leave for 10 minutes. Then sieve.
Drink 2 to 3 cups per day as needed.
Do not use during stomach ulcers.

11.5 Coriander

Coriandri, Fructus
Preparation: Different effects
Reduces inner wind. Tonifies and regulates stomach-qi. Directs wet heat and wetness cold out of the bladder. Eliminates wind-cold. Regulates and moves liver-qi.
3-6 g
Active ingredients: tannins, essential oil, vitamin C, sitosterol, protein
If measles or chickenpox have already broken out, do not use. Do not overdose.

11.6 Dandelion

Taraxaci
Preparation: Decoction
Reduces internal heat. Eliminates moisture-heat and heat-toxins. Dischars moisture. Supports spleen-qi and stomach-qi.
6-8 plants in two doses on an empty stomach for 10-14 days
Dosage: in case of liver and gall bladder problems and associated tension, nausea and irritability, decoction with 6-8 plants for 10-14 days in two doses on an empty stomach; with low milk production decoction from 10 plants in three doses on an empty stomach drink; for breast tumors and associated pain and swelling decoction drink from 20 plants in three doses on an empty stomach. Externally, the juice of the fresh plant acts as an antidote to snake bites.
Special features: In TCM, the dandelion due to its decongestant, decongestant and detoxifying effect as a remedy is of great importance in the treatment of disorders of the female reproductive organs, especially the breasts, as well as liver complaints. In addition, dandelion is very good to distribute the "hangover" the next morning after copious consumption of alcohol.
Do not use too much as it is easy to get diarrhea.

11.7 Fennel

Foeniculum vulgare
Preparation: Healing tea (infusion)
Strengthens the stomach energy, warms kidney energy and has an energizing effect.
Pour 3-5 grams of tea over with 250 ml of boiling water and leave for 10 minutes. Then sieve. Drink in three doses on an empty stomach
For the powder, roast the fennel in a dry pan until it starts to smell, then

grind it to a fine powder in a mortar or food processor; Add 1-5 g powder with boiling water and drink daily

Special Features: Fennel is one of the best remedy for physical weakness and lack of vitality due to inadequate or cold digestive energy that prevents

that the body absorbs enough nutrients and energy from food.

In rare cases, skin, stomach and intestinal reactions were observed.

Active ingredients: essential oil, trans-anethole, fenchone, fatty oil, protein, sugar.

11.8 St. Benedict's thistle, blessed thistle, holy thistle,

Centaurea benedicta

Preparation: Healing tea (infusion)

Strengthens and regulates stomach-Qi and intestinal Qi, transforms mucus and moisture, and conducts, clears toxic heat, lowers fever.

The Benedictine herb has a certain allergy potential. The oil of the plant, which was used in purulent skin ulcers, acts bacteriostatic especially against staphylococci.

11.9 Summer savory

Satureja hortensis

Preparation: Healing tea (infusion)

Tonifies kidney-yang, heart-qi, stomach- and spleen-qi and warms the middle, moves the liver-qi and blood, releases mucous

and cold from the lungs, opens the surface, induces wind-cold.

Pour 2 teaspoons of the tea into 250 ml of boiling water and leave for 10 minutes. Then sieve. Drink 2 to 3 cups per day as needed. (on www.ebns.at in the shop)

The herb with the peppery aroma makes hearty dishes wholesome, has a stomach-strengthening and antibacterial, soothing

and appetizing.

Ideal for preventing colds: strengthens the defense when drinking tea for 14 days. After enjoying raw food savory activates

the spleen yang.

Use: in legumes, soups, salads and as a tea (not in the evening), external use: softening and anti-inflammatory, in incontinence or nocturnal wetting (but not in children), for libido the savory in schnapps insert

The herb with the peppery aroma makes hearty dishes wholesome, has a stomach-strengthening and antibacterial, soothing

and appetizing.

11.10 Wormwood

Artemisia absinthium, herb.
Preparation: Healing tea (infusion)
Strengthens Spleen-Qi and Stomach-Qi, moves Liver-Qi, regulates bile flow, dissipating Moisture-Heat and Heat, regulating the uterus.
1 tsp. To 1 / 2l water
Vermouth - Not only used to eliminate worms; it is also a highly effective liver and digestive aid. He also helps to remove blockages that produce a lethargic menstruation. It is always best to take this herbal remedy in conjunction with other herbs.

Medical applications: anemia, arthritis, bloating, circulatory system, colds, constipation, depression, edema, earache, fever, gynecology, wind, gallbladder, gallstones, gout, heartburn, hepatitis, jaundice, kidney disease, morning sickness, nausea, obesity, parasites, Rheumatism, stomach ailments, worms.

Properties: Abortive, alterative, appetite promoting, wormer, antibiotic, anti-depressant, anti-inflammatory, antipyretic, antiseptic, aromatic, bittertonikum, anti-flatulence, cholagogue, digestive, menstrual enhancer, stomach-strengthening, wormer.
Do not use in pregnancy. It is always best to take this herbal remedy in conjunction with other herbs.

12 Basics of Nutrition

The basic principles of nutrition described herein are general recommendations. They are not aimed at a specific form of therapy. Recommendations concerning a therapy have priority.

12.1 Nutrition

Regular meals in a relaxed atmosphere. A warm breakfast is considered a good start into the day.
The main meals ought to be taken for lunch – supper in the early evening. Pay attention to feeling hungry or sated: don't eat too much nor remain hungry is the rule
Prepare the meals freshly from natural, regional products. Frozen, heat-conserved, industrially prepared or foodstuffs cooked in the microwave oven are rejected.
Choice of foodstuffs according to the season: more cooling food in summer, more warming food in winter.
Eat cooked food at least twice a day. Food and drinks ought to be lukewarm, never ice-cold or hot.
Raw vegetables, briefly cooked vegetables, freshly squeezed juices and mineral water are not recommended. Milk and dairy products are only included in the diet if they don't cause problems. Don't use therapeutic recipes over a longer period without consulting your doctor or therapist.

Varied food
Enjoy the diversity of foodstuffs. Characteristics of a balanced nutrition are variety, suitable combination and a balanced quantity of rich and low energy foodstuffs (on one hand avoiding undersupply with essential nutrients and on the other hand to take to many undesirable substances).

A lot of Cereal Products - and Potatoes
Bread, pasta, rice, cereal flakes (best wholemeal) as well as potatoes contain almost no fat, but many vitamins, mineral nutrients, trace elements, roughage and secondary plant substances. These foodstuffs ought to be taken with low-fat side dishes.

Vegetables and Fruit – „Take Five" every day ... 5 portions of vegetables and fruit a day, as fresh as possible, briefly cooked, or maybe one portion as a juice – ideal as a side dish to every meal as well as snack between meals: Thus a lot of vitamins, mineral nutrients as well as roughage and secondary plant substances

Daily milk and dairy products
Milk and Dairy Products every Day, once or twice per Week Fish;
meat, sausages as well as eggs moderately. These foodstuffs contain
valuable nutrients like calcium in the milk, iodine selenium and omega-3
fat acids in saltwater fish. Meat is favorable due to its high content of
disposable iron and the vitamins B1, B6 and B12. Quantities of 300 – 600
g meat and sausage per week are sufficient. Prefer low-fat products,
especially in meat- and dairy products.

Low-fat and fatty Foodstuffs
Fat supplies us with essential fat acids and fatty foodstuffs contain also
fat-soluble vitamins. Fat is high in energy; therefore much fat in the food
may cause overweight, possibly also cancer. Too many saturated fat
acids may further a tendency for cardio-vascular diseases in the long
term. Prefer vegetable oils and fats (e.g. rapeseed-, olive-, soya-oils and
solid fats produced therefrom). Beware of invisible fat in meat- and dairy
products, pastry and sweets as well as in fast-food and convenience
foods. 70 – 90 g fat per day is sufficient.

Moderately Sugar and Salt
Take sugar and foods/drinks containing various kinds of sugar (e.g.
glucose syrup) only occasionally. Use herbs and spices as well as a little
salt creatively. Prefer salt containing iodine.

Plenty of Liquids
Water is absolutely essential. Drink 1-2 l liquids every day. Prefer water
(with or without gas) and other low-calorie drinks. Alcoholic drinks should
not be taken.

Tasty Dishes, carefully cooked
Cook the meals with as low temperatures and as short as possible, using
little water and fat – this preserves the original taste, keeps the nutrients
intact and prevents the production of harmful compounds.

Take time and enjoy the food
Take your Time and enjoy your Food
Eating consciously helps to eat right. The eye enjoys food, too. It's fun,
invites to enjoy varied dishes and stimulates the feeling of satiety.

Watch your Weight and stay in Motion
A balanced diet and a lot of exercise and sport (30 – 60 min/day) are a
healthy combination. The right weight furthers well-being and health.
Thermals, directional effectiveness, digestive power
There are various criteria for judging the effectiveness of herbs and
foodstuffs.
The use of certain herbs and ingredients is based on observations of the
effects on the body which these foodstuffs, herbs and spices show after
having eaten them. The medical science has developed following system:
Every ingredient or herb has a directional effectiveness. Furthermore,
there are herbs which have a special effect on certain organs.
The basic condition for a healthy metabolism is to obtain sufficient energy
from food and that the digestive process doesn't use too much energy.
An easily digestible meal makes content and sated, doesn't cause
flatulence and fatigue after the meal. The perfect spices increase the
healthiness of our meals. Very often, just small doses of herbs and spices
will suffice. They are not used to make us sated, but to help our digestive
organs to digest the food.

12.2 Recipes

The recipes list the ingredients to be used and the cooking instructions
show how the dish is prepared. The list of ingredients shows the
concerned quantities as well as the relevance for the therapy. If you find
„less than mentioned", try to comply or find an alternative from the „list of
recommended foodstuffs". Mostly it shall result just in a small change of
taste when you simply avoid this ingredient.
Mild cooking methods: boiling, stewing, poaching, steaming
Strong cooking methods: barbecuing, roasting, frying, smoking
Balanced cooking methods: deep-frying, baking brick
Deep-freezing and warming in the microwave oven should be avoided
(denaturalization).

12.3 Foodstuffs

Foodstuffs have an effect on body and soul like medicinal herbs, only a
very much milder one. Dietary advice is mainly based on regional
foodstuffs. The knowledge about the effects of each foodstuff and the
knowledge, when which foodstuff shall be used, is based on the
orthodoschool of medicine. Use ecologic-organic products, if possible. As
everything should be cooked for a long time due to a better digestability
and very rarely eaten raw, the food agrees with everyone.

The classification of the foodstuffs according to their effect on the body is the basis in order to achieve a harmonious status of health.
Dietary advisors do not recommend certain foodstuffs for everyone. The individual diet is tailor-made for the individual constitution.

Buy only fresh and ripe fruit and vegetables. You ought to leave unripe fruit and vegetables and such with brown spots and wilted leaves behind in the market. In this case take deep-frozen goods (never ready-to-serve dishes!). Fruit and vegetables are deep-frozen immediately after harvesting and often contain more vitamins and minerals than the goods from the vegetable shelf. Whereas conserved or tinned goods contain very much less biological substances. Also, salt, sugar and others are mostly added to the latter. Never leave the foodstuffs in the water after washing them to avoid that many vital substances get drowned. Clean salads, fruit and vegetables immediately before serving.

Please make sure of the hygienic processing of foodstuffs. Clean your salads, fruit and vegetables carefully. When cooking with meat, prepare all ingredients first and then process the meat products. Clean the worktop and tools very carefully. Wooden surfaces ought to be treated with a mild disinfectant regularly in order to reduce germination.
Store fruit and vegetables separately, if possible. Harvested fruit and vegetables are still alive and emit e.g. ethylene gas, which makes other products ripen and age faster. Keep meat and fish in the closed packaging or store them in the fridge in closed containers.

12.4 Herbs

There are some basic rules for storing medicinal herbs. On principle, herbs must be protected from direct sunlight, humidity and heat.

Containers for the storage of herbs may be glasses, ceramic jars and even plastic containers. However, plastic is a rather unsuitable material and should only be a short-term solution. In case of glass containers, use a dark material.

Medicinal herbs cannot be kept for any long period. The shelf life of herbs is limited. However, it can be prolonged with suitable storage. The place should be dark, rather cool and absolutely dry. A wooden medicine cabinet, placed not directly next to a source of heat, would be ideal.

Never buy large quantities of herbs so as not to have to throw them away. Label the container with the name of the herb and the date of harvesting or processing.

13 Other dietic-books

The following syndromes of dietetics, TCM or for a therapy supplement for cancer are available.

Dietetics

E001. Nutrition of the infant - baby food
E002. Nutrition during lactation
E003. Nutrition in old age
E004. Nutrition of children and adolescents
E005. Nutrition of athletes
E006. Light weight
E007. Pregnancy
E008. Full food

Protein and electrolyte - kidneys
E009. (hemodialysis) dialysis treatment
E010. Acute renal failure
E011. Chronic renal insufficiency
E012. Nephrotic syndrome
E013. Kidney stones (nephrolithiasis)

Gastrointestinal tract - pancreas
E014. Acute pancreatitis (inflammation of the pancreas)
E015. Chronic pancreatitis (inflammation of the pancreas)

Gastrointestinal tract - small intestine and large intestine
E016. Acute obstipation (constipation)
E017. Chronic obstipation (constipation)
E018. Colon irritabile
E019. Diverticulitis
E020. Acquired lactose intolerance (lactose malabsorption)
E021. Fructose malabsorption
E022. Glutensensitive enteropathy (celiac disease)
E023. Colectomy
E024. Short Bowel Syndrome

Gastrointestinal tract - liver, gallbladder, bile ducts
E025. Acute and chronic hepatitis (inflammation of the liver)
E026. Cholelithiasis (bile stones)
E027. fatty liver
E028. cirrhosis

Gastrointestinal tract - Stomach and duodenal intestine
E029. Acute gastritis
E030. Chronic gastritis
E031. Stomach bleeding
E032. Ulcus ventriculi and duodenal ulcer
E033. Condition after gastric surgery

Gastrointestinal tract - oral cavity and esophagus
E034. Stomatitis
E035. Esophageal carcinoma (esophageal cancer)
E036. Refluosophagitis (heartburn)

Special diseases
E037. Phenylketonuria (PKU)
E038. Rheumatic joint diseases

Metabolism
E039. Obesity (overweight)
E040. Diabetes mellitus
E041. Eating disorders (underweight)

Fat metabolism
E042. Hypercholesterolaemia (increased cholesterol level)
E043. Hepatic Encephalopathy

Heart and circulation
E044. Arteriosclerosis (arterial calcification)
E045. Heart insufficiency
E046. Hypertension
E047. Hyperuricaemia and gout

Changed nutrient requirements
E048. In case of fever
E049. For malignant diseases
E050. After burns
E051. Radiation and chemotherapy

CANCER
E100. Pancreatic cancer
E101. Bladder cancer
E102. Blood cancer (leukemia)
E103. Breast cancer
E104. Colorectal cancer
E105. Gastric cancer
E106. Kidney cancer
E107. Esophageal cancer

TCM
E200. Bladder - moisture heat in the bladder
E201. Bladder - moisture and cold in the bladder
E202. Bladder - emptiness and cold in the bladder

E203. Large intestine - external cold affects the large intestine
E204. Large intestine - moisture heat in the large intestine
E205. Large intestine - heat blocks the intestine II acute
E206. Large intestine - dryness of the colon
E207. Large intestine - Yang deficiency (cold)
E208. Heart - Blood insufficiency
E209. Heart - Blood stagnation
E210. Heart - Fire
E211. Heart - Hot mucus clogs the heart pores
E212. Heart - Cold mucus clogs the heart pores
E213. Heart - Qi deficiency
E214. Heart - Yang deficiency
E215. Heart - Yin deficiency
E216. Liver - Ascending Liver Yang
E217. Liver - Blood deficiency
E218. Liver - Blood stagnation
E219. Liver - Moisture heat in liver and gall bladder
E220. Liver - Fire
E221. Liver - Gall bladder Qi-Empty
E222. Liver - Cold in the liver meridian
E223. Liver - Qi stagnation
E224. Liver - Wind
E225. Liver - Wind with ascending liver Yang
E226. Liver - Wind with blood anemic
E227. Liver - Wind with extreme heat
E228. Lung - Qi deficiency
E229. Lung - Mucus-moisture in the lungs
E230. Lung - Mucus-heat in the lungs
E231. Lung - Mucus-cold in the lungs
E232. Lung - Dryness of the lungs
E233. Lung - Wind-heat attacks the lungs
E234. Lung - Wind-cold affects the lungs
E235. Lung - Yin deficiency
E236. Stomach - Bloodstagnation
E237. Stomach - Fire
E238. Stomach - Cold with liquid
E239. Stomach - Nutrition stagnation
E240. Stomach - Qi deficiency
E241. Stomach - Rebellious Qi
E242. Stomach - Yin Emptiness
E243. Spleen - Heat and moisture attack the spleen
E244. Spleen - Coldness and moisture affects the spleen
E245. Spleen - Qi deficiency
E246. Spleen - Qi deficiency + Declining spleen Qi
E247. Spleen - Qi deficiency + spleen does not control the blood
E248. Spleen - Yang deficiency
E249. Kidney - Heart and kidney no longer communicate
E250. Kidney - Jing deficiency
E251. Kidney - Kidneys cannot receive the Qi
E252. Kidney - Qi is not stable
E253. Kidney - Yang deficiency
E254. Kidney - Yin deficiency

For further information visit nutribook.info.

14 EBNS - Software for nutritional counseling

The main task of the database is to create personalized nutritional advice for each patient individually. The database was developed for Dietetics and Traditional Chinese Medicine.
The Database supports training and advices in the daily work routine.

The computer program provides lists of recipes, ingredients and herbs, which are given to the client. individually adjustable according to patient's request from whole food to vegetarians (lacto, ovo, ...). For every register there is an information sheet which can be given to the client. All texts can be individually designed.

The syndromes can be combined and result in an intersection of the recommended recipes and ingredients. The automated diagnosis for the TCM enables you to check your experience during the training as well as to confirm your diagnosis in the working day. You select several predefined symptoms and have the program automatically display the relevant syndromes.

How to work with the database:
Select the patient / client, select one or more of the syndromes you diagnosed and print the folder.

You can change all values, create new symptoms or syndromes, develop recipes, change or adapt ingredients and herbs to your findings. In simple client management, all relevant data about the person is stored. You get an overview of the past diagnoses and the development of the course of the disease.

As a consultant you save a lot of time when you print out the recipe, food and herbal lists for the recognized syndromes and give them to the clients. You can use this time for a personal conversation. With the database, dieticians and nutritionists can view the nutrients and trace elements for each recipe and develop recipes for syndromes even with suggested ingredients.

All recipe and grocery lists can also be ordered from me as a combination of several diseases. I wish all readers good luck, health and happiness in life.
More information can be found at www.ebns.at.
Volunteer: www.krebsinfo.at
Josef Miligui